6

FRINGE

Cut a piece of cardboard 3" x 6½". Wind the yarn **loosely** and **evenly** around the cardboard lengthwise until the card is filled, then cut across one end; repeat as needed.
Hold together as many strands as specified in individual instructions; fold in half.
With **wrong** side facing and using a crochet hook, draw the folded end up through a row and pull the loose ends through the folded end ***(Fig. 2a)***; draw the knot up **tightly *(Fig. 2b)***. Repeat in each row across short edge of Rug.
Lay flat on a hard surface and trim the ends.

Fig. 2a

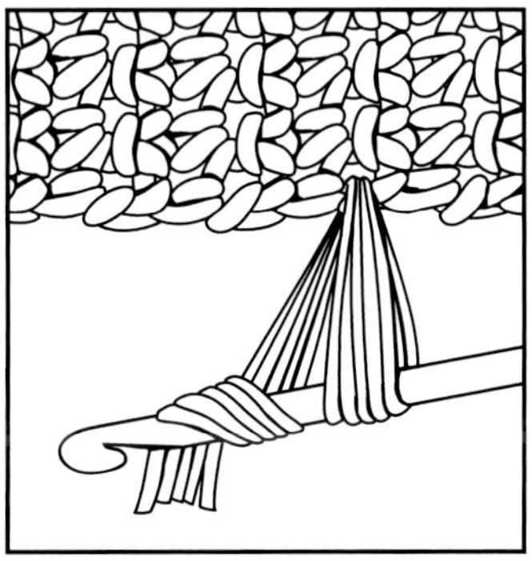

Fig. 2b

Production Team: Instructional Editor - Sarah J. Green; Technical Editor - Linda Luder; Artist - Faith Lloyd; Senior Artist - Diana Sanders; and Photo Stylist - Lori Dimond.

1. ROUND RAG-LOOK

Shown on page 10.

Finished Size: 41" diameter

MATERIALS

Worsted Weight Yarn:
- Lt Blue - 14 ounces, (400 grams, 790 yards)
- Blue - 12 ounces, (340 grams, 680 yards)
- Ecru - 7 ounces, (200 grams, 395 yards)

Crochet hook, size N (9.00 mm) **or** size needed for gauge

Each round is worked holding three strands of yarn together.

GAUGE SWATCH: Rnds 1-4 = 8½" diameter

RUG

Rnd 1 (Right side)**:** With two strands of Ecru and one strand of Lt Blue, ch 3, 10 hdc in third ch from hook; join with slip st to top of beginning ch-3: 11 sts.

Note: Loop a short piece of yarn around any stitch to mark Rnd 1 as **right** side.

Rnd 2: Ch 3 **(counts as first dc, now and throughout)**, dc in same st, 2 dc in next hdc and in each hdc around; join with slip st to first dc: 22 dc.

Rnd 3: Ch 3, dc in same st and in next dc, (2 dc in next dc, dc in next dc) around; join with slip st to first dc: 33 dc.

Rnd 4: Ch 3, dc in next dc, 2 dc in next dc, (dc in next 2 dc, 2 dc in next dc) around; join with slip st to first dc, finish off: 44 dc.

Rnd 5: With **right** side facing and using two strands of Blue and one strand of Ecru, skip first 4 dc and join yarn with slip st in next dc; ch 3, dc in same st and in next 3 dc, (2 dc in next dc, dc in next 3 dc) around; join with slip st to first dc, finish off: 55 dc.

Rnd 6: With **right** side facing and using one strand of **each** color, skip first 3 dc and join yarn with slip st in next dc; ch 3, dc in same st and in next 4 dc, (2 dc in next dc, dc in next 4 dc) around; join with slip st to first dc, finish off: 66 dc.

Rnd 7: With **right** side facing and using two strands of Lt Blue and one strand of Blue, skip first 3 dc and join yarn with slip st in next dc; ch 3, dc in same st and in next 5 dc, (2 dc in next dc, dc in next 5 dc) around; join with slip st to first dc, finish off: 77 dc.

Rnd 8: With **right** side facing and using two strands of Blue and one strand of Lt Blue, skip first 4 dc and join yarn with slip st in next dc; ch 3, dc in same st and in next 6 dc, (2 dc in next dc, dc in next 6 dc) around; join with slip st to first dc, do **not** finish off: 88 dc.

Rnd 9: Ch 3, dc in next 3 dc, 2 dc in next dc, (dc in next 7 dc, 2 dc in next dc) around to last 3 dc, dc in last 3 dc; join with slip st to first dc, finish off: 99 dc.

Rnd 10: With **right** side facing and using two strands of Lt Blue and one strand of Blue, skip first 8 dc and join yarn with slip st in next dc; ch 3, dc in same st and in next 8 dc, (2 dc in next dc, dc in next 8 dc) around; join with slip st to first dc, finish off: 110 dc.

Rnd 11: With **right** side facing and using one strand of **each** color, skip first 5 dc and join yarn with slip st in next dc; ch 3, dc in same st and in next 9 dc, (2 dc in next dc, dc in next 9 dc) around; join with slip st to first dc, finish off: 121 dc.

Rnd 12: With **right** side facing and using two strands of Lt Blue and one strand of Ecru, skip first 5 dc and join yarn with slip st in next dc; ch 3, dc in same st and in next 10 dc, (2 dc in next dc, dc in next 10 dc) around; join with slip st to first dc, finish off: 132 dc.

Rnd 13: With **right** side facing and using two strands of Ecru and one strand of Lt Blue, skip first 6 dc and join yarn with slip st in next dc; ch 3, dc in same st and in next 11 dc, (2 dc in next dc, dc in next 11 dc) around; join with slip st to first dc, do **not** finish off: 143 dc.

Rnd 14: Ch 3, dc in next 4 dc, 2 dc in next dc, (dc in next 12 dc, 2 dc in next dc) around to last 7 dc, dc in last 7 dc; join with slip st to first dc, finish off: 154 dc.

Rnd 15: With **right** side facing and using two strands of Lt Blue and one strand of Ecru, skip first 10 dc and join yarn with slip st in next dc; ch 3, dc in same st and in next 13 dc, (2 dc in next dc, dc in next 13 dc) around; join with slip st to first dc, finish off: 165 dc.

Rnd 16: With **right** side facing and using one strand of **each** color, skip first 8 dc and join yarn with slip st in next dc; ch 3, dc in same st and in next 14 dc, (2 dc in next dc, dc in next 14 dc) around; join with slip st to first dc, finish off: 176 dc.

Rnd 17: With **right** side facing and using two strands of Lt Blue and one strand of Blue, skip first 6 dc and join yarn with slip st in next dc; ch 3, dc in same st and in next 15 dc, (2 dc in next dc, dc in next 15 dc) around; join with slip st to first dc, finish off: 187 dc.

Rnd 18: With **right** side facing and using two strands of Blue and one strand of Lt Blue, skip first 8 dc and join yarn with slip st in next dc; ch 3, dc in same st and in next 16 dc, (2 dc in next dc, dc in next 16 dc) around; join with slip st to first dc, do **not** finish off: 198 dc.

Rnd 19: Ch 3, dc in next 6 dc, 2 dc in next dc, (dc in next 17 dc, 2 dc in next dc) around to last 10 dc, dc in last 10 dc; join with slip st to first dc, do **not** finish off: 209 dc.

Rnd 20: Ch 1, 2 sc in same st, sc in each dc around; join with slip st to first sc: 210 sc.

Rnd 21: Ch 2, skip next sc, ★ slip st in next sc, ch 2, skip next sc; repeat from ★ around; join with slip st to joining slip st, finish off.

3

2

2. BORDERED RECTANGLE

Shown on page 6.

Finished Size: 26" x 38"

MATERIALS

Worsted Weight Yarn:
Lt Brown - 8 ounces, (230 grams, 450 yards)
Burgundy - 4½ ounces, (130 grams, 255 yards)
Green - 4½ ounces, (130 grams, 255 yards)
Brown - 4½ ounces, (130 grams, 255 yards)
Lt Green - 4¼ ounces, (120 grams, 240 yards)
Rose - 4 ounces, (110 grams, 225 yards)
Crochet hooks, sizes K (6.50 mm) **and** N (9.00 mm) **or** sizes needed for gauge

Each row is worked holding three strands of yarn together in the following color combinations:

MC: Use one strand **each** of Burgundy, Green, and Brown.
Color A: Use one strand **each** of Rose, Lt Green, and Lt Brown.
Color B: Use one strand of Lt Green and 2 strands of Lt Brown.
Color C: Use one strand of Rose and 2 strands of Lt Brown.

GAUGE: With larger size hook, 10½ sc and 11½ rows = 6"

Gauge Swatch: 6¼" square
With larger size hook and MC, ch 12.
Row 1: Sc in second ch from hook and in each ch across: 11 sc.
Rows 2-12: Ch 1, turn; sc in each sc across. Finish off.

RUG BODY

With larger size hook and MC, ch 46.

Row 1 (Wrong side)**:** Sc in second ch from hook and in each ch across: 45 sc.

Note: Loop a short piece of yarn around **back** of any stitch on Row 1 to mark **right** side.

Rows 2-6: Ch 1, turn; sc in each sc across.

To change colors, work the last sc to within one step of completion, hook new yarn ***(Fig. 3)*** and draw through both loops on hook. Do **not** carry yarn across back of work. Use separate balls of MC for each edge of Rug. Leave yarn ends and dropped colors on **wrong** side of work. Use dropped colors on the next row unless otherwise indicated.

Fig. 3

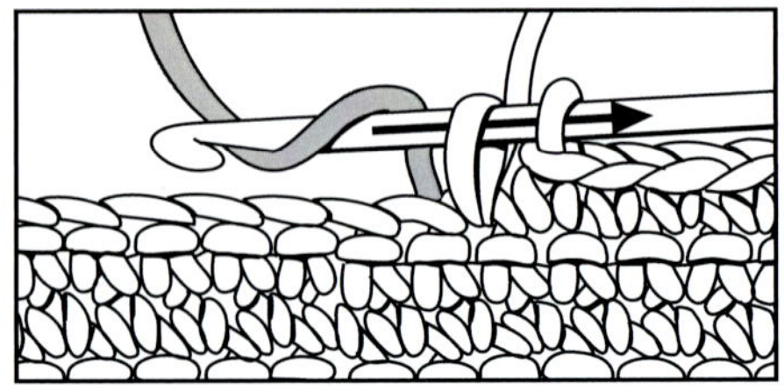

Row 7: Ch 1, turn; sc in first 6 sc changing to Color A in last sc made, sc in next 33 sc changing to MC in last sc made, sc in last 6 sc.

Continue to change colors in same manner.

Row 8: Ch 1, turn; sc in first 6 sc; with Color A sc in next 33 sc, cut Color A; with MC sc in last 6 sc.

Row 9: Ch 1, turn; sc in first 6 sc; with Color B sc in next 33 sc; with MC sc in last 6 sc.

Row 10: Ch 1, turn; sc in first 6 sc; with Color B sc in next 33 sc, cut Color B; with MC sc in last 6 sc.

Row 11: Ch 1, turn; sc in first 6 sc; with Color A sc in next 33 sc; with MC sc in last 6 sc.

Row 12: Ch 1, turn; sc in first 6 sc; with Color A sc in next 33 sc, cut Color A; with MC sc in last 6 sc.

Row 13: Ch 1, turn; sc in first 6 sc; with Color C sc in next 33 sc; with MC sc in last 6 sc.

Row 14: Ch 1, turn; sc in first 6 sc; with Color C sc in next 33 sc, cut Color C; with MC sc in last 6 sc.

Row 15: Ch 1, turn; sc in first 6 sc; with Color A sc in next 33 sc; with MC sc in last 6 sc.

Rows 16-67: Repeat Rows 8-15, 6 times; then repeat Rows 8-11 once **more**.

Row 68: Ch 1, turn; sc in first 6 sc, cut MC; with Color A sc in next 33 sc, cut Color A; with MC sc in last 6 sc.

Rows 69-74: Ch 1, turn; sc in each sc across; at end of Row 74, do **not** finish off.

Edging: With smaller size hook and working in end of rows, ch 1, slip st in first row, ch 1, skip next row, (slip st in next row, ch 1, skip next row) across; with larger size hook and working in free loops of beginning ch ***(Fig. 1, page 1)***, (slip st, ch 1) twice in ch at base of first sc, (skip next ch, slip st in next ch, ch 1) across to last 2 chs, skip next ch, (slip st, ch 1) twice in last ch; with smaller size hook and working in end of rows, skip first row, slip st in next row, ch 1, (skip next row, slip st in next row, ch 1) across; with larger size hook and working in sts across Row 74, (slip st, ch 1) twice in first sc, (skip next sc, slip st in next sc, ch 1) across to last 2 sc, skip next sc, (slip st, ch 1) twice in last sc; join with slip st to first slip st, finish off.

---

3. HORIZONTAL STRIPES

Shown on page 5.

Finished Size: 26½" x 37½"

MATERIALS

Worsted Weight Yarn:
- Tan - 17¾ ounces, (500 grams, 1,005 yards)
- Rose - 6¼ ounces, (180 grams, 355 yards)
- Green - 5½ ounces, (160 grams, 310 yards)

Crochet hook, size N (9.00 mm) **or** size needed for gauge

Each row is worked across length of Rug Body holding three strands of yarn together. When joining yarn and finishing off, leave a 6" end to be worked into fringe.

GAUGE: In pattern, sc, (ch 1, sc) 5 times and 10 rows = 5¼"

Gauge Swatch: 5¼" square
With Tan, ch 12.
Work same as Rug Body for 10 rows.

RUG BODY

With Tan, ch 80.

Row 1 (Right side)**:** Sc in second ch from hook, ★ ch 1, skip next ch, sc in next ch; repeat from ★ across; finish off: 40 sc and 39 ch-1 sps.

Note: Loop a short piece of yarn around any stitch to mark Row 1 as **right** side.

Row 2: With **wrong** side facing, join Rose with sc in first sc ***(see Joining With Sc, page 1)***; (ch 1, sc in next sc) across; finish off.

Row 3: With **right** side facing, join Green with sc in first sc; (ch 1, sc in next sc) across; finish off.

Row 4: With **wrong** side facing, join Rose with sc in first sc; (ch 1, sc in next sc) across; finish off.

Row 5: With **right** side facing, join Tan with sc in first sc; (ch 1, sc in next sc) across; finish off.

Row 6: With **wrong** side facing, join Green with sc in first sc; (ch 1, sc in next sc) across; finish off.

Row 7: With **right** side facing, join Tan with sc in first sc; (ch 1, sc in next sc) across; finish off.

Row 8: With **wrong** side facing, join Rose with sc in first sc; (ch 1, sc in next sc) across; finish off.

Row 9: With **right** side facing, join Green with sc in first sc; (ch 1, sc in next sc) across; finish off.

Row 10: With **wrong** side facing, join Rose with sc in first sc; (ch 1, sc in next sc) across; finish off.

Row 11: With **right** side facing, join Tan with sc in first sc; (ch 1, sc in next sc) across; finish off.

Row 12: With **wrong** side facing, join Tan with sc in first sc; (ch 1, sc in next sc) across; finish off.

Row 13: With **right** side facing, join Tan with sc in first sc; (ch 1, sc in next sc) across; finish off.

Row 14: With **wrong** side facing, join Green with sc in first sc; (ch 1, sc in next sc) across; finish off.

Rows 15-17: Repeat Rows 11-13.

Row 18: With **wrong** side facing, join Rose with sc in first sc; (ch 1, sc in next sc) across; finish off.

Rows 19-42: Repeat Rows 11-18, 3 times.

Rows 43-51: Repeat Rows 3-11.

TRIM

FIRST SIDE

With **right** side facing, join Tan with slip st in first sc on Row 51; slip st in next ch-1 sp, (ch 1, slip st in next ch-1 sp) across, slip st in last sc; finish off.

SECOND SIDE

With **right** side facing, working in free loops ***(Fig. 1, page 1)*** and in sps across beginning ch, join Tan with slip st in first ch; slip st in next sp, (ch 1, slip st in next sp) across, slip st in next ch; finish off.

Holding 3 strands of corresponding color yarn together, add additional fringe ***(Figs. 2a & b, page 3)***.

5

1

4. BRAIDED LOOK

Shown on Front Cover.

Finished Size: 26½" x 37½"

MATERIALS

Worsted Weight Yarn:
- Rust - 8¾ ounces, (250 grams, 495 yards)
- Blue - 8¼ ounces, (235 grams, 465 yards)
- Purple - 7¼ ounces, (210 grams, 410 yards)
- Burgundy - 6¼ ounces, (180 grams, 355 yards)
- Lt Blue - 4¼ ounces, (120 grams, 240 yards)
- Peach - 2 ounces, (60 grams, 115 yards)

Crochet hook, size N (9.00 mm) **or** size needed for gauge

Each row is worked across length of Rug Body holding three strands of yarn together. When joining yarn and finishing off, leave a 6" end to be worked into fringe.

GAUGE: In pattern, 10 sts and 14 rows = 5¼"

Gauge Swatch: 4¾"w x 5¼"h
With Rust, ch 10.
Work same as Rug Body for 14 rows.

RUG BODY

With Rust, ch 72.

Row 1 (Right side)**:** Slip st in second ch from hook, (sc in next ch, slip st in next ch) across; finish off: 71 sts.

Note: Loop a short piece of yarn around any stitch to mark Row 1 as **right** side.

Row 2: With **wrong** side facing, join Purple with sc in first slip st ***(see Joining With Sc, page 1)***; (slip st in next sc, sc in next slip st) across; finish off.

Row 3: With **right** side facing, join Burgundy with slip st in first sc; (sc in next slip st, slip st in next sc) across; finish off.

Row 4: With **wrong** side facing, join Blue with sc in first slip st; (slip st in next sc, sc in next slip st) across; finish off.

Row 5: With **right** side facing, join Lt Blue with slip st in first sc; (sc in next slip st, slip st in next sc) across; finish off.

Row 6: With **wrong** side facing, join Blue with sc in first slip st; (slip st in next sc, sc in next slip st) across; finish off.

Row 7: Repeat Row 3.

Row 8: With **wrong** side facing, join Purple with sc in first slip st; (slip st in next sc, sc in next slip st) across; finish off.

Row 9: With **right** side facing, join Rust with slip st in first sc; (sc in next slip st, slip st in next sc) across; finish off.

Row 10: Repeat Row 8.

Rows 11-13: Repeat Rows 3-5.

Row 14: With **wrong** side facing, join Rust with sc in first slip st; (slip st in next sc, sc in next slip st) across; finish off.

Row 15: With **right** side facing, join Peach with slip st in first sc; (sc in next slip st, slip st in next sc) across; finish off.

Row 16: With **wrong** side facing, join Rust with sc in first slip st; (slip st in next sc, sc in next slip st) across; finish off.

Rows 17 and 18: Repeat Rows 5 and 6.

Row 19: With **right** side facing, join Purple with slip st in first sc; (sc in next slip st, slip st in next sc) across; finish off.

Row 20: With **wrong** side facing, join Burgundy with sc in first slip st; (slip st in next sc, sc in next slip st) across; finish off.

Row 21: With **right** side facing, join Rust with slip st in first sc; (sc in next slip st, slip st in next sc) across; finish off.

Row 22: Repeat Row 20.

Row 23: Repeat Row 19.

Row 24: Repeat Row 6.

Rows 25-27: Repeat Rows 17-19.

Rows 28-30: Repeat Rows 14-16.

Row 31: Repeat Row 19.

Row 32: Repeat Row 6.

Rows 33 and 34: Repeat Rows 3 and 4.

Row 35: Repeat Row 21.

Rows 36-69: Repeat Rows 2-35.

TRIM

FIRST SIDE

With **right** side facing, join Rust with slip st in first slip st on Row 69; ★ ch 1, skip next sc, slip st in next slip st; repeat from ★ across; finish off.

SECOND SIDE

With **right** side facing and working in free loops of beginning ch ***(Fig. 1, page 1)***, join Rust with slip st in first ch; ★ ch 1, skip next ch, slip st in next ch; repeat from ★ across; finish off.

Holding 2 strands of corresponding color yarn together, add additional fringe ***(Figs. 2a & b, page 3)***.

---

5. CHECK PATTERN

Shown on page 9.

Finished Size: 23" x 36"

MATERIALS

Worsted Weight Yarn:
Blue - 15 ounces, (430 grams, 850 yards)
Ecru - 12¼ ounces, (350 grams, 690 yards)
Crochet hook, size N (9.00 mm) **or** size needed for gauge

Each row is worked across length of Rug Body holding three strands of yarn together. When joining yarn and finishing off, leave a 6" end to be worked into fringe.

GAUGE: In pattern, 9 sts and 10 rows = 5"
10½ sc and 11½ rows = 6"
Gauge Swatch: 6¼" square
With Blue, ch 12.
Row 1: Sc in second ch from hook and in each ch across: 11 sc.
Rows 2-12: Ch 1, turn; sc in each sc across. Finish off.

RUG BODY

With Blue, ch 66.

Row 1 (Right side)**:** Sc in second ch from hook and in each ch across; finish off: 65 sc.

Note: Loop a short piece of yarn around any stitch to mark Row 1 as **right** side.

Row 2: With **wrong** side facing, join Ecru with sc in first sc ***(see Joining With Sc, page 1)***; ch 1, (skip next st, sc in next sc, ch 1) 3 times, ★ skip next st, sc in next 7 sc, ch 1, (skip next st, sc in next sc, ch 1) 3 times; repeat from ★ across to last 2 sc, skip next sc, sc in last sc; finish off.

Row 3: With **right** side facing, join Blue with sc in first sc; working in **front** of next ch, dc in st one row **below**, (sc in next sc, working in **front** of next ch, dc in st one row **below**) 3 times, ★ sc in next 7 sc, working in **front** of next ch, dc in st one row **below**, (sc in next sc, working in **front** of next ch, dc in st one row **below**) 3 times; repeat from ★ across to last sc, sc in last sc; finish off.

Rows 4-9: Repeat Rows 2 and 3, 3 times.

Row 10: With **wrong** side facing, join Ecru with sc in first sc; sc in each st across; finish off: 65 sc.

Row 11: With **right** side facing, join Blue with sc in first sc; sc in next 7 sc, ch 1, (skip next st, sc in next st, ch 1) 3 times, ★ skip next st, sc in next 7 sc, ch 1, (skip next st, sc in next st, ch 1) 3 times; repeat from ★ 2 times **more**, skip next sc, sc in last 8 sc; finish off.

Row 12: With **wrong** side facing, join Ecru with sc in first sc; ★ sc in next 7 sc, working **behind** next ch, dc in st one row **below**, (sc in next sc, working **behind** next ch, dc in st one row **below**) 3 times; repeat from ★ across to last 8 sc, sc in last 8 sc; finish off.

Rows 13-18: Repeat Rows 11 and 12, 3 times.

Row 19: With **right** side facing, join Blue with sc in first sc; sc in each st across; finish off: 65 sc.

Rows 20-45: Repeat Rows 2-19 once, then repeat Rows 2-9 once **more**.

TRIM

FIRST SIDE

With **right** side facing, join Blue with slip st in first sc on Row 45; ★ ch 1, skip next st, slip st in next st; repeat from ★ across; finish off.

SECOND SIDE

With **right** side facing and working in free loops of beginning ch ***(Fig. 1, page 1)***, join Blue with slip st in first ch; ★ ch 1, skip next ch, slip st in next ch; repeat from ★ across; finish off.

Holding 3 strands of corresponding color yarn together, add additional fringe ***(Figs. 2a & b, page 3)***.

8

7

6. DOTTED STRIPES

Shown on page 2.

Finished Size: 25½" x 37½

MATERIALS

Worsted Weight Yarn:
White - 18½ ounces, (530 grams, 1,045 yards)
Green - 5½ ounces, (160 grams, 310 yards)
Pink - 5½ ounces, (160 grams, 310 yards)
Lavender - 5½ ounces, (160 grams, 310 yards)
Crochet hook, size N (9.00 mm) **or** size needed for gauge

Each row is worked across length of Rug Body holding three strands of yarn together. When joining yarn and finishing off, leave a 6" end to be worked into fringe.

GAUGE: In pattern, 11 sts and 12 rows = 6"

Gauge Swatch: 6" square
With White, ch 12.
Work same as Rug Body for 12 rows.

RUG BODY

With White, ch 70.

Row 1 (Right side)**:** Sc in second ch from hook and in each ch across; finish off: 69 sc.

Note: Loop a short piece of yarn around any stitch to mark Row 1 as **right** side.

Row 2: With **wrong** side facing, join White with sc in first sc ***(see Joining With Sc, page 1)***; ★ ch 1, skip next sc, sc in next sc; repeat from ★ across; finish off: 35 sc and 34 chs.

Row 3: With **right** side facing, join Green with sc in first sc; ★ working **behind** next ch, dc in st one row **below**, sc in next sc; repeat from ★ across; finish off: 69 sts.

Row 4: With **wrong** side facing, join Green with sc in first sc; ★ ch 1, skip next dc, sc in next sc; repeat from ★ across; finish off: 35 sc and 34 chs.

Row 5: With **right** side facing, join White with sc in first sc; ★ working **behind** next ch, dc in dc one row **below**, sc in next sc; repeat from ★ across; finish off: 69 sts.

Row 6: With **wrong** side facing, join White with sc in first sc; ★ ch 1, skip next dc, sc in next sc; repeat from ★ across; finish off: 35 sc and 34 chs.

Row 7: With **right** side facing, join Pink with sc in first sc; ★ working **behind** next ch, dc in dc one row **below**, sc in next sc; repeat from ★ across; finish off: 69 sts.

Row 8: With **wrong** side facing, join Pink with sc in first sc; ★ ch 1, skip next dc, sc in next sc; repeat from ★ across; finish off: 35 sc and 34 chs.

Row 9: With **right** side facing, join White with sc in first sc; ★ working **behind** next ch, dc in dc one row **below**, sc in next sc; repeat from ★ across; finish off: 69 sts.

Row 10: With **wrong** side facing, join White with sc in first sc; ★ ch 1, skip next dc, sc in next sc; repeat from ★ across; finish off: 35 sc and 34 chs.

Row 11: With **right** side facing, join Lavender with sc in first sc; ★ working **behind** next ch, dc in dc one row **below**, sc in next sc; repeat from ★ across; finish off: 69 sts.

Row 12: With **wrong** side facing, join Lavender with sc in first sc; ★ ch 1, skip next dc, sc in next sc; repeat from ★ across; finish off: 35 sc and 34 chs.

Row 13: With **right** side facing, join White with sc in first sc; ★ working **behind** next ch, dc in dc one row **below**, sc in next sc; repeat from ★ across; finish off: 69 sts.

Row 14: With **wrong** side facing, join White with sc in first sc; ★ ch 1, skip next dc, sc in next sc; repeat from ★ across; finish off: 35 sc and 34 chs.

Rows 15-49: Repeat Rows 3-14 twice, then repeat Rows 3-13 once **more**.

Row 50: With **wrong** side facing, join White with sc in first sc; sc in each st across; finish off.

TRIM

FIRST SIDE

With **right** side facing, join White with slip st in first sc on Row 50; ★ ch 1, skip next sc, slip st in next sc; repeat from ★ across; finish off.

SECOND SIDE

With **right** side facing and working in free loops of beginning ch ***(Fig. 1, page 1)***, join White with slip st in first ch; ★ ch 1, skip next ch, slip st in next ch; repeat from ★ across; finish off.

Holding 3 strands of corresponding color yarn together, add additional fringe ***(Figs. 2a & b, page 3)***.

7. STRIPED WEAVE

Shown on page 14.

Finished Size: 24½" x 36½"

MATERIALS

Worsted Weight Yarn:
- Green - 8¾ ounces, (250 grams, 495 yards)
- Ecru - 6½ ounces, (185 grams, 365 yards)
- Lt Rose - 6½ ounces, (185 grams, 365 yards)
- Black - 4 ounces, (110 grams, 225 yards)
- Rose - 3¼ ounces, (90 grams, 185 yards)

Crochet hook, size N (9.00 mm) **or** size needed for gauge

Each row is worked across length of Rug Body holding three strands of yarn together. When joining yarn and finishing off, leave a 6" end to be worked into fringe.

GAUGE: In pattern, sc, (ch 1, sc) 5 times and 11 rows = 5¼"

Gauge Swatch: 5¼" square
With Green, ch 12.
Work same as Rug Body for 11 rows.

RUG BODY

With Green, ch 78.

Row 1 (Right side)**:** Sc in second ch from hook and in next ch, ch 1, ★ skip next ch, sc in next ch, ch 1; repeat from ★ across to last 3 chs, skip next ch, sc in last 2 chs; finish off: 40 sc and 37 ch-1 sps.

Note: Loop a short piece of yarn around any stitch to mark Row 1 as **right** side.

Row 2: With **wrong** side facing, join Black with sc in first sc ***(see Joining With Sc, page 1)***; ch 1, (sc in next ch-1 sp, ch 1) across to last 2 sc, skip next sc, sc in last sc; finish off: 39 sc and 38 ch-1 sps.

Row 3: With **right** side facing, join Green with sc in first sc; sc in next ch-1 sp, (ch 1, sc in next ch-1 sp) across, sc in last sc; finish off: 40 sc and 37 ch-1 sps.

Row 4: With **wrong** side facing, join Ecru with sc in first sc; ch 1, (sc in next ch-1 sp, ch 1) across to last 2 sc, skip next sc, sc in last sc; finish off: 39 sc and 38 ch-1 sps.

Row 5: With **right** side facing, join Lt Rose with sc in first sc; sc in next ch-1 sp, (ch 1, sc in next ch-1 sp) across, sc in last sc; finish off: 40 sc and 37 ch-1 sps.

Row 6: With **wrong** side facing, join Rose with sc in first sc; ch 1, (sc in next ch-1 sp, ch 1) across to last 2 sc, skip next sc, sc in last sc; finish off: 39 sc and 38 ch-1 sps.

Row 7: With **right** side facing, join Lt Rose with sc in first sc; sc in next ch-1 sp, (ch 1, sc in next ch-1 sp) across, sc in last sc; finish off: 40 sc and 37 ch-1 sps.

Row 8: With **wrong** side facing, join Ecru with sc in first sc; ch 1, (sc in next ch-1 sp, ch 1) across to last 2 sc, skip next sc, sc in last sc; finish off: 39 sc and 38 ch-1 sps.

Row 9: With **right** side facing, join Green with sc in first sc; sc in next ch-1 sp, (ch 1, sc in next ch-1 sp) across, sc in last sc; finish off: 40 sc and 37 ch-1 sps.

Row 10: With **wrong** side facing, join Black with sc in first sc; ch 1, (sc in next ch-1 sp, ch 1) across to last 2 sc, skip next sc, sc in last sc; finish off: 39 sc and 38 ch-1 sps.

Row 11: With **right** side facing, join Green with sc in first sc; sc in next ch-1 sp, (ch 1, sc in next ch-1 sp) across, sc in last sc; finish off: 40 sc and 37 ch-1 sps.

Rows 12-51: Repeat Rows 4-11, 5 times.

TRIM

FIRST SIDE

With **right** side facing, join Green with slip st in first sc on Row 51; ch 1, (slip st in next ch-1 sp, ch 1) across to last 2 sc, skip next sc, slip st in last sc; finish off.

SECOND SIDE

With **right** side facing, working in free loops ***(Fig. 1, page 1)*** and in sps across beginning ch, join Green with slip st in first ch; ch 1, (slip st in next sp, ch 1) 37 times, skip next ch, slip st in next ch; finish off.

Holding 3 strands of corresponding color yarn together, add additional fringe ***(Figs. 2a & b, page 3)***.

8. RAG-LOOK SQUARES

Shown on page 13.

Finished Size: 26½" x 39½"

MATERIALS

Worsted Weight Yarn:
- Green - 19 ounces, (540 grams, 1,075 yards)
- Ecru - 12 ounces, (340 grams, 680 yards)

Crochet hook, size N (9.00 mm) **or** size needed for gauge

Yarn needle

Each round is worked holding three strands of yarn together.

GAUGE: One Square = 6½"

Gauge Swatch: 3¾" square
Work same as Square through Rnd 3.

STITCH GUIDE

DECREASE A (uses next sp and next sc)
Pull up a loop in next sp and in next sc, YO and draw through all 3 loops on hook.

DECREASE B (uses next sc and next sp)
Pull up a loop in next sc and in next sp, YO and draw through all 3 loops on hook.

SQUARE (Make 15)

Rnd 1 (Wrong side)**:** Using two strands of Ecru and one strand of Green, ch 2, (sc, ch 2) 4 times in second ch from hook; join with slip st to first sc: 4 sc and 4 ch-2 sps.

Note: Loop a short piece of yarn around **back** of any stitch on Rnd 1 to mark **right** side.

Rnd 2: Ch 1, ★ (sc, ch 2, sc) in next ch-2 sp, ch 1; repeat from ★ around; join with slip st to first sc: 8 sps.

Rnd 3: Ch 1, ★ (sc, ch 2, sc) in next ch-2 sp, ch 1, sc in next ch-1 sp, ch 1; repeat from ★ around; join with slip st to first sc, finish off: 12 sps.

Rnd 4: With **right** side facing and using two strands of Green and one strand of Ecru, join yarn with sc in any corner ch-2 sp ***(see Joining With Sc, page 1)***; ch 2, sc in same sp, ch 1, (sc in next ch-1 sp, ch 1) twice, ★ (sc, ch 2, sc) in next corner ch-2 sp, ch 1, (sc in next ch-1 sp, ch 1) twice; repeat from ★ 2 times **more**; join with slip st to first sc: 16 sps.

Rnd 5: Ch 1, ★ (sc, ch 2, sc) in next ch-2 sp, ch 1, (sc in next ch-1 sp, ch 1) 3 times; repeat from ★ around; join with slip st to first sc, finish off: 20 sps.

Rnd 6: With **wrong** side facing and using three strands of Green, join yarn with sc in any corner ch-2 sp; ch 2, sc in same sp, ch 1, (sc in next ch-1 sp, ch 1) 4 times, ★ (sc, ch 2, sc) in next corner ch-2 sp, ch 1, (sc in next ch-1 sp, ch 1) 4 times; repeat from ★ 2 times **more**; join with slip st to first sc, finish off: 24 sps.

ASSEMBLY

Forming 3 strips of 5 Squares each, whipstitch Squares together as follows:
Place two Squares with **wrong** sides together. Using two strands of Green and beginning in second ch of first corner ch-2, sew through both pieces once to secure the beginning of the seam, leaving an ample yarn end to weave in later. Working through **both** loops of each st of **both** pieces, insert the needle from front to back through first st and pull yarn through ***(Fig. 4)***, ★ insert the needle from front to back through next st and pull yarn through; repeat from ★ across, ending in first ch of next corner ch-2.
Whipstitch strips together in same manner.

Fig. 4

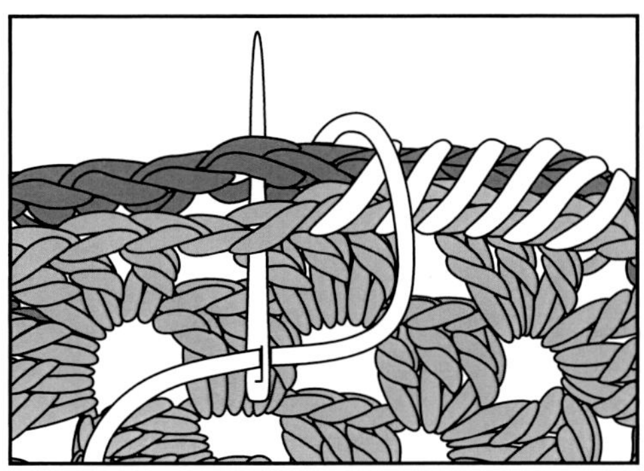